ZOOS AND GAME RESERVES

© Aladdin Books Ltd 1988

Designed and produced by
Aladdin Books Ltd
70 Old Compton Street
London W1V 5PA

*First published in the
United States in 1988 by*
Gloucester Press
387 Park Avenue South
New York, NY10016

ISBN 0-531-17090-X

Design Rob Hillier
Editor Catherine Bradley
Researcher Cecilia Weston-Baker
Illustrator Ron Hayward Associates

Printed in Belgium

All rights reserved

Library of Congress Catalog
Card Number: 87-82889

The front cover shows a tiger in Royal Chitawan National Park, Nepal.
The back cover shows elephants at London Zoo.

*The author, Miles Barton, has worked as an academic researcher on
animal welfare and animals in captivity. He is now a producer at the
BBC's natural history unit.*

*The consultant, Dr Andrew Kitchener, is a zoologist at the University
of Reading, U.K. He is also a committee member of the Cat Survival
Trust, which breeds endangered cats in captivity.*

Contents

ZOOS AND GAME RESERVES

Miles Barton

Gloucester Press
New York : London : Toronto : Sydney

Introduction

Every year 350 million people visit nearly 750 zoos worldwide. However, some people believe that keeping animals in captivity is wrong and that zoos are cruel. They argue that television can inform and educate the public about animals. They also say that the millions of dollars spent on zoos would be better spent on saving the wilderness in which animals live.

In defense of zoos, most zoo directors emphasize their research, conservation and educational activities. They argue that there is no substitute for the sight and even smell of an animal in front of you.

▽ Tourists watch a group of elephants from a lodge in the Tsavo National Park in Kenya. Although it is best to go and see animals in the wild, not everyone can afford to do this. Zoos provide an opportunity to see the animals close up and find out more about them.

Keeping an animal in a zoo means that people can be shown how it lives as well as being made aware of what is needed to preserve it in the wild. Raising public awareness about wildlife is one of the most important functions of zoos.

As the human population continues to expand, game reserves and national parks will be the only places where animals can be seen in the wild. Like zoos, they will have to provide good facilities for animals and people alike and encourage the preservation of the wildlife. In the future there will be less and less difference between good zoos and game reserves.

Prisons and pits

The old idea of a zoo was simply a menagerie or collection of animals in a viewing pit. Exotic animals were exhibited in the barest of surroundings so that visitors had a clear view of them. Animals were there to be stared at, marveled at and often laughed at with no thought of where they came from or how they behaved in the wild. Nowadays more progressive zoos spend a lot of money on the animals' welfare.

Humans have kept animals in captivity for thousands of years. The ancient Egyptians kept menageries of baboons and lions in their temples. In Central America the Aztec ruler, Montezuma, had a collection of eagles, jaguars, llamas and snakes, looked after by 300 keepers.

▽ Cats like this ocelot in Quito, Ecuador can become bored easily in captivity. In the wild they range long distances through the forest in search of prey. In a cage like this they pace back and forth along the same path and may develop strange weaving motions because of boredom.

Animals were also used by kings, queens and politicians to exchange as gifts. The German Emperor Frederick II swapped a polar bear for a giraffe with the Sultan of Egypt. Similar exchanges of wild animals still take place. In the 1970s, China gave giant pandas to France, the United States and Britain as gifts.

The Romans scoured the world for strange beasts, keeping some in menageries while others met a more barbaric fate at the hands of gladiators. Men were forced to fight lions, tigers, bears and even crocodiles. This kind of mass killing for entertainment has stopped. But there are still zoos throughout the world, where wild animals are used to provide a spectacle without any regard for the animals' welfare.

▷ Brown bears are intelligent animals which in the wild travel long distances to find a variety of food. In zoos they need climbing areas, scratching posts, toys to play with and secluded dens. Yet in bad zoos they are still kept in small concrete pits with nothing to do but beg for food.

"The cost of keeping all the rare animals in zoos is at least $15 million a year."

Colin Rawlins,
The Zoological Society of London

The ideal zoo

In an ideal zoo all the animals are born in captivity and have not had to make the huge adjustment to loss of freedom experienced by wild animals. Their welfare is put before the needs of keepers or visitors. They are displayed in natural family groups and provided with the space and furnishings they need to behave as they do in the wild. The ideal zoo concentrates on animals which it can maintain in the best possible conditions and makes special efforts to breed those which are threatened in the wild.

Many zoos follow these ideas. More attention is paid to the design of cages and enclosures and researchers look into new ways of making the occupants happy. Many zoos are now able to breed animals in captivity. In 1964 the percentage of captive born rare animals in zoos was 36 per cent but by 1987 it was nearly 75 per cent. Some animals bred in zoos, such as the Pere David's deer, have been saved from extinction and returned to the wild. It takes a long time for animals to adjust to the wild.

Zoos like the ones in San Diego and in Jersey in Great Britain have led the way in the imaginative display and breeding of endangered species from geckoes to gorillas.

"Ultimately zoos may provide the last refuge for many species of animals which face extinction in the wild."

Colin Rawlins,
The Zoological Society of London

▷ In 1965 there were no captive bred cheetahs in zoos but now over half of those in zoos were born in captivity. It was discovered at Whipsnade Zoo in England that adult cheetahs would not breed if kept together all the time. By mating them once or twice a year, Whipsnade has bred nearly 120 cubs in 20 years.

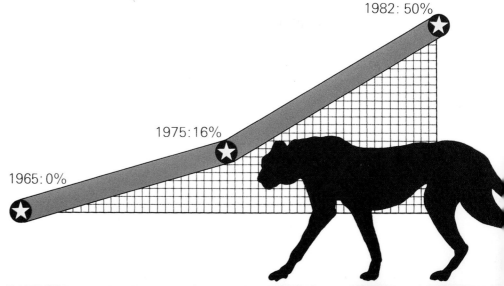

1982: 50%

1975: 16%

1965: 0%

Some people feel there is no such thing as an ideal zoo and that wild animals in captivity will always suffer from a lack of freedom. But animals in the wild are never free from fear of predators, parasites, disease and starvation. A good zoo cannot provide a natural habitat but it should recreate as many of its beneficial features as possible while giving extra protection from harmful ones. Thus monkeys are given climbing frames which allow them to climb as they would in the jungle.

△ The Wolf is a social animal that lives and hunts in a pack. At Port Lympne Zoo in England, the Canadian timber wolves are kept in a group, in an enclosure which includes a small woods similar to the wild. There are also secluded dens where mothers can raise their pups. There is enough space for individuals to avoid each other should tensions develop within the pack.

▷ In 1965 only 13 per cent of black rhinos in zoos were captive bred. Now the figure is nearer 50 per cent. Black rhinos can be aggressive to future mates and need careful handling when introduced. They can be kept in pairs but the male must be removed before calving because he may injure the baby.

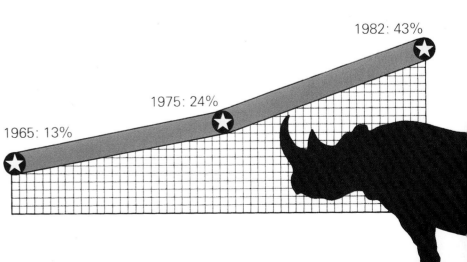

1982: 43%

1975: 24%

1965: 13%

SURVIVAL **PROFILE...**

Happy captives

Some animals are easier to keep in zoos than others. Social plant eaters such as zebras, deer and antelope live in groups and are happy to spend their time feeding. Zoo personnel are also beginning to realize that the smaller animals, whose worlds are easier to recreate, can provide exciting exhibits. Given the right setting, the very active marmots will create an entire "town" on a grassy bank with sentries on lookout, adults digging or feeding and babies playing or suckling all day long.

> **The meerkat**
> The meerkat is a small mongoose measuring about 60cm (2ft) from head to tail. It lives in groups of 10 to 20 animals in burrows in the dry rocky areas of southern Africa. It feeds on insects, birds and their eggs, rats, lizards and snakes.

△ Meerkats are now very popular in zoos because they adapt well to life in captivity and a family group provides an interesting attraction. They are active during the day and spend much of their time playing. A family group is made up of a breeding pair, a litter of 2-5 babies and one or two young to help with the rearing of their brothers and sisters. One of the group acts as a sentry to warn of any dangers. All they need is a small enclosure with rocks and bushes for cover and a source of heat.

▷ Giraffes have been kept and bred in zoos since the 1830s. They are very docile and easy to handle. All they require is a supply of twigs and hay, provided at the right height so they can digest their food naturally. They have very long tongues for feeding and grooming. If they are kept in family groups, they will not get bored and will happily feed all day.

The giraffe
It stands up to 580cm (19ft) high and weighs up to 800kg (1,760 lbs). Both sexes have short horns. It lives in family groups of 5-10. A 60kg (132 lb) baby giraffe is born after 450 days in the womb. It can live up to 28 years.

The San Diego mountain king snake
It is less than 100cm (40in) in length and feeds on small birds, lizards, mice and other snakes. Mating takes place in the spring and the female lays 3-6 eggs a month later. It likes to hide under rocks.

△ Attractively colored snakes such as this San Diego mountain king snake can do much to dispel the often groundless fears many have of snakes. All it needs is a small heated cage with a stone to hide under and a regular supply of freshly killed mice. Snakes are bred in special hatcheries in some zoos and visitors can watch tiny reptiles emerge from eggs.

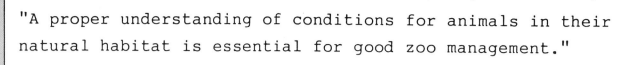

"A proper understanding of conditions for animals in their natural habitat is essential for good zoo management."

Trevor Scott
Director of the World Society for the Protection of Animals

12

Boredom

△ A llama takes children for a ride in London Zoo. Camels are also used for rides and elephants are taken for regular walks through the zoo to help them keep fit.

Many zoos are now looking at different ways of preventing boredom. One controversial way is to train animals to perform or give rides. This was stopped in the past because it was regarded as degrading but it is now used for the animals' benefit. Indeed Basle Zoo in Switzerland has a circus ring for the elephants and the keepers say the animals are healthier for it.

Training can also be used to demonstrate an animal's natural abilities. Birds of prey are rarely kept in cages big enough to fly in. But by training the bird to fly back to the lure using the age old art of falconry, the public is entertained and the bird exercised. Many zoos now have falconry displays or use parrots in a similar way.

An animal can also be kept active by making it work for food. This might simply involve hiding nuts so that monkeys have to search for them or putting mealworms in sand so foxes have to dig for their food. There are also more technological methods available. Monkeys have been trained to play electronic games in return for rewards.

◁ The great apes, regarded as most like us, have been given a range of human gadgets from slide projectors to electric organs to play with. In some zoos gorillas can even watch television.

Preventing extinction

△ The panda is one of the rarest large mammals. Pandas have only bred in three zoos outside their native China. Some 20 pandas have been born at Peking Zoo but only nine have survived. London Zoo went to great lengths in trying to breed its pandas. It even flew its female, Chi Chi, to meet a male, An An, in Moscow but the attempt was a failure. Female pandas are fertile for only a few days each year and as they are solitary by nature, it is very difficult to get a pair together at the best time for mating.

Some rare animals like Przewalski's horse and the Arabian oryx have been saved from extinction by being bred in captivity. Fortunately they were easy to breed in zoos unlike some other animals. For example, it is very difficult to get pandas, polar bears and elephants to mate and rear young successfully in captivity.

Because of the small numbers available, some zoo species have been allowed to breed with close relatives, which often has harmful effects. To avoid inbreeding, zoos now cooperate in having studbooks on computer and animals are moved between zoos to create new breeding groups. The result is healthier animals being born.

Modern scientific techniques are also used. Artificial insemination, where the sperm of the male is artificially placed in the female, has been performed on a number of zoo animals including gorillas, chimpanzees and pumas.

	population in zoos	population in wild
⭐ Przewalski's horse	552	0
⭐ Mauritius kestrel	10	6
⭐ Pink pigeon	48	18
⭐ Arabian oryx	*323	30
⭐ Pere David's deer	*1,500	40
⭐ Whooping crane	52	92
⭐ Rodriguez flying fox	51	100
⭐ Round island gecko	120	125
⭐ Pampas deer	42+	150
⭐ Golden lion tamarin	368	200
⭐ Asiatic lion	149+	280
⭐ Barren ground grizzly bear	6	500
⭐ Giant panda	15	1,000
⭐ Lion-tailed macaque	328+	1,000
⭐ Indian rhinoceros	76+	1,000
⭐ Sumatran tiger	213	1,000
⭐ Bengal tiger	59	2,500

* = reintroduced to the wild

△ The last herd of Arabian oryx in the wild was wiped out in 1972. However the Phoenix Zoo in Arizona had formed a captive herd 10 years earlier. In 1982 and 1984 groups of captive bred oryxes (totalling 20) were released in central Oman. They are now successfully breeding.

▷ A comparison of the numbers of some of the world's rarest species in zoos and in the wild demonstrates the importance of captive breeding. Many are familiar with the pandas and tigers but what about the even rarer pink pigeon and the Round Island gecko?

"Animals in captivity suffer from stress and like humans they can also die from it."

Bill Travers, Zoo Check

Aquariums

◁ Killer whales are the principal attraction of the modern aquarium, such as this one in Vancouver, Canada. Killer whales are the largest of all the dolphins. They are expensive to keep because they can eat 40 to 50kg (88-110 lbs) of fish a day. They need to be kept in large tanks to give them the space to swim properly. But while tanks are built so that visitors get a good view, does living in the pool satisfy the needs of this intelligent animal?

The sight of a killer whale swimming with a pair of sunglasses on its head is anything but natural, and yet performances like these draw enormous crowds and make aquariums profitable. But it is difficult to see how the small sterile pools in which whales and dolphins are kept can compare with the freedom they experience in the open sea. The stress of performing can lead to gastric ulcers. Dolphins in the oceans can live up to 30 years but in captivity their life expectancy is much lower. Although this is now rising and captive births are also becoming more common, many believe these creatures should not be kept in captivity.

Modern aquariums are very successful at recreating sections of the coral reef and the ocean floor. Tanks can hold hundreds or even thousands of tons of water. The artificial seawater is prepared by adding chemicals to ordinary water which is then heated to the correct temperature. Filters then clean the water and oxygen is added as it is circulated. Although marine fish can be seen behaving naturally, they are only rarely bred. New fish have to be imported from the wild.

▽ Bottle-nosed dolphins are sociable animals and form strong relationships with their keepers, whom they are always eager to please.

Better in the wild?

Some animals are better suited to captivity than others. In general, boredom is more of a problem in the carnivores, which in the wild may roam great distances in search of their prey. The keeping of polar bears in zoos has been much criticized, as they suffer from boredom and become aggressive. Leopards and smaller cats often develop strange behavior in captivity. Providing company will not solve this problem since they are by nature solitary animals.

The world of a bird of prey is a vast three dimensional one which is almost impossible to recreate successfully in a cage.

"An animal like a polar bear or an elephant shouldn't be in a zoo at all."

Virginia McKenna, Zoo Check

△ A recent survey of polar bears in British zoos revealed that over a half showed abnormal weaving movements. They need more space than they get in a zoo in which to roam. Some zoo directors now admit that their enclosures are unsuitable for keeping polar bears in captivity.

Perhaps zoos should only keep certain animals if there are very strong conservation reasons. Also, zoos should have to demonstrate that they have the facilities to provide for all of the animals' needs.

Sometimes captive breeding is not the best way of saving a particular species. Often the best way of protecting a creature is to set up a reserve within its natural habitat. In the case of the California condor well over $25m has been spent on captive breeding. Many people are asking what is the point of saving the condor if it will never fly free again?

△ There are 27 California condors in captivity and none in the wild. With such a small population it will be very difficult to build up a healthy stock in the future. Even if the zoos do succeed, it is unlikely that the birds will be returned to the wild.

Safari parks

In the last 20 years safari parks have sprung up around the world from Florida to Tokyo and from Sao Paulo in Brazil to Windsor in Britain. They cater to city dwellers who want a taste of the wild. The main feature of such parks is that it is the people who are confined, usually in a car, and the animals are free to wander around them. Anyone can drive past enclosures of lions, tigers and baboons. Entire African landscapes (without the carnivores) are recreated with zebra, elands and giraffe grazing peacefully as they would in the wild. Some parks confine the visitors in trains or cable cars on which they can travel past hippos floating in a pool or chimpanzees living on an island.

▽ Britain's first safari park opened at Longleat in Wiltshire, where lions roaming free on the grounds of a stately home in the English countryside rapidly caught the public imagination. Longleat started with just lions and many people thought they would escape or die of cold in the English winter. But they thrived and other parks rapidly followed their example.

Although the animals appear to have more space and freedom, safari parks still have their problems. Animals such as lions and tigers are kept in greater numbers than they would live in naturally. So the keepers must always be watching out for bullying. Indeed some members of the group may not get their fair share of food and it is difficult to spot and treat sick animals. In the past such parks were generally linked to circuses or fun fairs and because they kept only the more common and more spectacular animals, little attention was paid to education and conservation. This is now changing to some extent with zoos adopting the better aspects of safari parks and vice versa.

▽ In the San Diego Wild Animal Park the visitors are confined to an observation point overlooking grazing lands in a scene reminiscent of the East African plains. The animals are undisturbed by the people who have an excellent view from their high vantage point.

"We are faced with stark alternatives. Either we breed in captivity the ever increasing number of animal species threatened with extinction in the wild, or they vanish forever."
Elspeth Huxley, Author

21

Game reserves

Game reserves were areas set aside for the hunting of game animals. Today game reserves and national parks are often the last remaining areas of true wilderness. But, in Africa and Asia, it is difficult to prevent herders from bringing in their hungry cattle and goats. Poaching is another problem; a hunter can earn more than a year's wages by killing a rhino for its horn. This makes poaching difficult to stop.

Farming and poaching are just two of the problems facing reserves and national parks throughout the world. In the United States and Europe, demands for land for housing have led to the encroachment on national parks. But these parks are also important for preserving wildlife.

△ Guillemots and puffins (with orange feet) on the Pribilof Islands off Alaska. These islands are a sanctuary, where birds can live undisturbed.

▽ Tourists in Kenya are eager to see the great cats, such as this leopard. But cars can destroy fragile vegetation. Animals with cubs may be disturbed or they may be prevented from successfully killing their prey. Also cars may drive a cat into the path of other cats who will kill it.

Managing the parks and reserves causes its own set of problems. In some, the numbers of elephants have risen dramatically, leading to damage of the vegetation on which the other animals depend. To secure the reserves' long term future, some African countries have decided to keep down the number of elephants, arguing that it is better to be shot than to starve.

However, another way to prevent overpopulation (and also inbreeding) is to move surplus animals to other parks, as has been done successfully with white rhinos. As the human population grows and the reserves and national parks shrink, their animals will be subject to more and more human interference.

▽ A black rhino lies dead, having been killed for its horn in the Masai Mara Reserve in Kenya, September 1984. Despite being protected within national parks, their numbers are dwindling. Kenya and Tanzania have the largest population with only 3,700 black rhinos.

What price wildlife?

As the pressure on game reserves and national parks intensifies, so they will be increasingly expected to pay their way. It is easier to persuade governments and farmers that parks are necessary if they make money. To meet tourists' demands, large areas of wilderness have been put aside for animals. This works as long as it is carefully controlled and both animals and people benefit from the arrangement.

More controversially countries such as Zimbabwe and South Africa allow surplus animals to be shot either by rich, foreign trophy hunters or by local people to provide meat. If trophy hunting is strictly controlled, the killing of small numbers of lions, buffalo, elephants and even rhino can generate enormous amounts of money. This can be used to maintain the parks and protect thousands of animals.

The use of reserves for tourism requires greater human intervention such as the laying of roads to prevent excessive damage to vegetation by tourist vehicles. Some parks have been recreated by humans from farmland, with animals brought in from the wild and the large predators kept out. They are like an enormous safari park.

The Pilanesberg National Park
In South Africa this park was laid out in an area settled by farmers, where animals had disappeared. People were moved out and a total of 5,965 animals of 20 species were introduced between 1979 and 1984. Sixteen species have become established, including ostriches, white and black rhinos, giraffes and wildebeests.

▽ The 200 or so Manchurian or Japanese cranes left in Japan are now protected in a national park established in the Kushiro swamp on Hokkaido. The crane's elegance and the fact that it is Japan's national bird make it an important tourist attraction.

"No large wild terrestrial animal will persist long into the future unless cared for in some way by man."

William Conway,
The New York
Zoological Society

Game reserves and parks are also chosen as the first step in reintroducing captive bred animals to the wild. Knowledge about animal behavior gained in zoos is particularly important at this stage. Cross-fostering or the placing of the eggs of a rare bird in the nest of a more common, related species has been used successfully to reintroduce Whooping cranes to the wild using Sandhill cranes as foster parents.

△ Yellowstone is probably the most famous national park in the United States. Its bears are unafraid of the visitors which makes for excellent photographs. But they can become dangerous when they decide to investigate tents or cars in search of food.

The Serengeti

The Serengeti National Park in Tanzania has been described as the greatest wildlife spectacle on earth. Herds of Thomson's gazelles, wildebeests and impala mingle with zebras, giraffes and warthogs providing food for both the large predators such as lions, leopards, cheetahs and hyenas as well as scavenging jackals and vultures. Tourists can visit the Serengeti to see animals in their natural state and pay for the upkeep of the park.

> **The wildebeest**
> It may reach a height of 145cm (4ft 10in) and weigh up to 290kg (638 lbs). Males are some 20 per cent larger and heavier than females. Calves are born after 8 months in the womb and can stand within minutes.

△ Groups of wildebeests are a common sight in the Serengeti. Each year herds of up to 400,000 animals travel from the Serengeti in the south to the plains of the Masai Mara in the north where they calve. Many do not survive the journey. Calves are born in January or February at the beginning of the rainy season, so there is plenty of grass to eat. Lions and hyenas feast on the calves but they are unable to kill them all. Adult males and females have horns which they use to defend themselves and their young.

The African hunting dog

It stands 70cm (28 in) high and weighs about 18-28kg (40-62lbs). They range over an area as large as 1,000 sq km (400 sq miles) but stay put to rear the pups. Up to 16 are born in a burrow.

◁ Wild dogs live in packs of up to 30 animals. They feed mainly on the herds of Thomson's gazelle and impala. They are efficient hunters.

The African elephant

They are the largest living land mammals standing up to 11.8ft high and weighing up to 13,200 lbs. Males are larger than females. A single baby is born after 22 months in the womb. They can live for 70 years.

▽ Elephant herds can be made up of females and their young or young males. Old males are solitary. They feed on roots, leaves, fruit and bark which is picked off trees with their trunks. Elephants bathe daily and the mothers wash their babies. They defend their young aggressively. They are very sociable and have recently been found to communicate using low-pitched sounds which humans cannot hear. If one of the herd is ill, the others will support it. Poaching for the ivory tusks remains a serious problem. Game reserves provide some protection from poachers.

Zoo 2001

As the wilderness shrinks due to pressure from agriculture and more and more people live in cities, zoos and wildlife parks will become even more important. Africans today are more likely to see an elephant in a zoo or a game reserve than in the wild.

But we need to change the way zoos are run. There must be fewer of them and their animals' lives must be made as interesting and natural as possible. More zoos will concentrate on keeping smaller creatures. Many of these less spectacular but equally interesting animals are also in need of saving from extinction. Cooperation between zoos will develop with more exchanges between zoos for breeding purposes. More captive bred animals will be returned, if not to the wild, at least to parks and reserves. Some people believe that test tube baby technology will be used to save endangered species, although it has only been successful in a handful of cases so far.

Between them, zoos and game reserves will encourage people to care more about the wild animals that share our planet and preserve as wide a range of species as possible for future generations.

▷ This baby zebra was removed as an embryo from its real mother and placed inside this Welsh pony who gave birth to and reared it. In the future this technique may be used to breed an endangered species, so that a single mother can have many babies instead of just one.

▽ In the future perhaps humans will be confined while animals such as this olive baboon will go free.

"Can we seriously contemplate a world without elephants, rhinoceros, Arabian oryx or a multitude of other creatures large and small?"

Roger Wheater, The Zoological Society of Scotland, Zoo Director

Hard facts

Endangered animals living in zoos

Birds
Black-necked crane
Hawaiian goose
White-winged wood duck
Mauritius pink pigeon

Carnivores
African hunting dog
Asiatic lion
Clouded leopard
Giant panda
Maned wolf
Margay
Siberian tiger
Snow leopard
Sumatran tiger

Hoofed mammals
Addax
Arabian gazelle
Arabian oryx
Banteng
Barasingha or Swamp deer
Formosan sika deer
Gaur
Grevy's zebra
Hartmann's mountain zebra
Lechwe waterbuck
Markhor
Onager
Pere David's deer
Przewalski's horse
Pygmy hippopotamus
Scimitar-horned oryx
Wisent or European bison

Monkeys and apes
Barbary macaque
Cotton-top tamarin
Goeldi's monkey
Golden lion tamarin
Lion-tailed macaque
Orangutan

Small mammals
Black lemur
Brush-tailed bettong
Mongoose lemur
Red-fronted lemur

A good zoo guide

Great Britain
Jersey Zoo
London Zoo, Regent's Park
Marwell Zoo, Hampshire
Whipsnade Zoo, Bedfordshire

Europe
Alpenzoo, Innsbruck, Austria
Basle Zoo, Switzerland
Frankfurt Zoo, W Germany
Royal Rotterdam Zoological
    Gardens, the Netherlands

Walsrode Bird Park,
    Rieselbach, W Germany
West Berlin Zoo and
    Aquarium, W Germany

North America
Arizona-Sonora Desert Museum
Bronx Zoo, New York
Brookfield Zoo, Chicago, Illinois
Metro Toronto Zoo, Ontario,
    Canada
Monkey Jungle, Miami, Florida

National Zoo, Washington DC
Philadelphia Zoo,
    Pennsylvania
San Diego Zoo and Wild
    Animal Park, California

Other
Peking Zoo, China
Taronga Zoo, Sydney,
    Australia
Zoo Negara, Kuala Lumpur,
    Malaysia

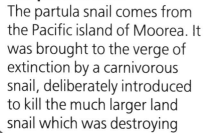

The partula snail
The partula snail comes from the Pacific island of Moorea. It was brought to the verge of extinction by a carnivorous snail, deliberately introduced to kill the much larger land snail which was destroying crops. Unfortunately the carnivorous snail developed a taste for the partula. It is now thought to be the rarest snail in the world and captive snails are being bred in lunch boxes in zoos throughout Europe.

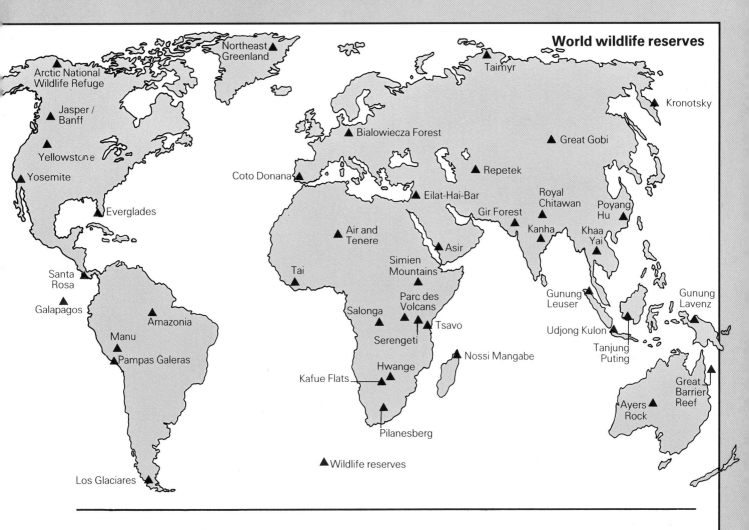

Northeast Greenland

Arctic National Wildlife Refuge

Taimyr

Kronotsky

Jasper / Banff

Yellowstone

Bialowiecza Forest

Great Gobi

Yosemite

Coto Donana

Repetek

Everglades

Eilat-Hai-Bar

Royal Chitawan

Poyang Hu

Gir Forest

Kanha

Khaa Yai

Santa Rosa

Air and Tenere

Asir

Galapagos

Tai

Simien Mountains

Gunung Leuser

Gunung Lavenz

Manu

Amazonia

Salonga

Parc des Volcans

Tsavo

Udjong Kulon

Tanjung Puting

Pampas Galeras

Serengeti

Nossi Mangabe

Kafue Flats

Hwange

Ayers Rock

Great Barrier Reef

Pilanesberg

Los Glaciares

▲ Wildlife reserves

Zoo success stories

The ne-ne or Hawaiian goose

Because it had no enemies on the islands where it lived, the Hawaiian goose flies only poorly. The introduction of domestic animals by man in the 18th century led to its rapid decline and by 1950 there were only 30 left in the wild. Today there is a wild population of about 750 birds, backed up by a captive bred population of about 1,300 so the species' survival is assured.

Pere David's deer

These were named after a French missionary in 1871. Some deer were sent to zoos in Europe from the last remaining herd in China. In 1900 the herd was wiped out. The Duke of Bedford collected as many of the remaining deer as possible in England where they bred easily. Today the world herd stands at 1,500. In the 1970s deer were returned to zoos in China but it was not until 1987 that 40 were finally released in the wild.

Przewalski's horse or Mongolian wild horse

Named after the Russian explorer who discovered it, the horse is the only surviving wild horse. From 1898-1903 44 animals were caught on the Russian steppes and shipped to zoos in the West. The wild population was wiped out by hunting and by the late 1940s the last horse was taken from the wild. Despite initial failures at breeding there are now more than 500 wild horses in zoos.

Index

Photographic Credits:
Cover: Coleman; pages 4-5 and 19: Survival Anglia; pages 6, 10, 13, 23, 25, 28-29 and back cover: Bruce Coleman; pages 7, 14 and 16: Robert Harding Libary; page 8-9: Port Lympne Zoo/Sue Duff; pages 11 (both), 17, 22, 23, 26 and 27 (both): Planet Earth; page 12: Twycross Zoo: pages 15 and 28: London Zoo; page 18: Zoo Check; pages 20 and 21: Ardea; pages 22 and 24-25: Zefa; page 30: Flora and Fauna Preservation Society.

PRINTED IN BELGIUM BY
proost
INTERNATIONAL BOOK PRODUCTION